Selections from the
Bible

(The New Testament)
(Rendered into simple English)

O.P. GHAI
with a Foreword by
Fr. T.V. Kunnunkal

New Dawn

NEW DAWN
An imprint of Sterling Publishers (P) Ltd.
A-59 Okhla Industrial Area, Phase-II,
New Delhi-110020.
Tel: 26387070, 26386209
Fax: 91-11-26383788 E-mail: ghai@nde.vsnl.net.in
www.sterlingpublishers.com

Selections from the Bible
© 2003, Sterling Publishers Private Limited
ISBN 978-81-207-9459-7

Published by Sterling Publishers Pvt. Ltd., New Delhi-110020.
Lasertypeset by Vikas Compographics, New Delhi-110020.
Printed at Sai Printers, New Delhi-110020.

Contents

Foreword

Three major world religions, namely Judaism, Christianity and Islam, have several things in common: faith and practices centred around ethical norms and laws, the nature of God and His relations with people and world views resulting from these. Neither narrowly nor country based, these have found adherents all over the world, particularly Christianity and Islam. Yes, the zeal of the followers to spread their faith to others through gentle, and at times, not so gentle means, helped, no doubt in this. However, in the case of Buddhism, Jainism and especially Hinduism, the large underpinning for religion was provided by the culture of the people so that religion and culture became closely interlinked.

The series that Mr. O.P.Ghai has authored, focuses attention, on certain fundamental unity of various religions, in spite of differences. There are many points of confluence, if not congruence, between the world views of different religions, be it Hinduism or Christianity or any other religion. These find expression and articulation in the different scriptures. The role of suffering and its mystery, the presence of evil and the faith perspective, the idea of salvation or liberation, the means to attain such salvation, the role of sacraments and ethical life or sanskara, and ways and approaches to establish contact with the ultimate Reality, with God, through meditation, etc., *(sadhana)* are mentioned in the various scriptures.

The Bible (which literally means the book) is considered the Word of God by Christians. However, as Christian theologians would point out, there is a dual authorship of the various books of the Bible: on the one hand, the human author, conditioned by his times, his culture, education and background which are clearly reflected in his writing and which make it a truly human document and hence prone to error and, on the other hand, the divine author or the Word of God and His message, which He inspires the author to put down. Scriptural inspiration is a special miracle or grace given to the authors, who wrote the various books of the Bible. There are several factual errors in the Bible, the contribution of the human author. However, the inerrancy of the Bible refers to the truth revealed by God through the human author.

The Good News (which is what the word Gospel means) from God, brought to man, through Jesus, the Son of God, as written by the four authors and the letters by Paul and others, contain certain core teachings of Jesus. Jesus, born and brought up as a Jew, dared to challenge the status quo, the religious and ethical norms and traditions prevailing at His time, (often distortions of the original laws). He presented to the people a set of reorganized priorities, changed the emphasis from the outer to the inner, from reciting many prayers to praying in one's heart, pointed out the necessity to practise removal of materialism from the spirit, namely detachment of the heart from the wordly possessions, and above all, invited His followers to join together in building the human community of man, in love and fellowship, patterned on the divine community of God, the Father, the Son and the Holy Spirit, the three persons of the Trinity, but one God. So radical and so different was His life and teachings that while it attracted many followers, it also provoked the wrath of the powers that be, who managed to have Him killed. Yet, as the Gospel points out, He laid down His life, of His own will, as a sacrifice – for atonement of the sins of the world. Though as a human, He could die, Jesus, the Son of God, rose from the dead. He wanted His followers to share in His mission of building a new earth, new people and a new community. He set before them this challenge of beginning an establishment of the Kingdom of God, a communitarian task and a mission, which would endure for eternity in all its fullness.

Mr. Ghai has taken excerpts of the important passages from the four Gospels and the letters, which would provide the reader an initiation into the Bible. Taken out of context, some of passages may seem strange, but then, the World of God is like a double edged sword, and it can cut and enter in all directions. This great labour of love and devotion by the author, bringing the essence of various religions to the readers, is a most welcome initiative and most timely. It comes into our world of doubt and darkness, of cruel deeds and lack of kindness as gentle reminders that God still inspires men and women to light His paths and point His ways to others. I pray that Mr. Ghai may be richly blessed by God.

Thomas V. Kunnunkal

Preface

My interest in and love for sacred writings date back to the year 1930 when I, as a student, would read and recite the Japji, the great Sikh scripture, in the religious instruction class of my school. After passing the matriculation examination in 1934, I bought a copy of the Bhagavad Gita, the Hindu epic, and read it several times to be able to understand its divine message.

It was in 1938 that a friend of mine, knowing my religious leanings, presented me with a copy of the Bible which I used to read once in a while. The book created in me an urge to study the complete Holy Bible.

My next ten years were devoted to the teaching profession and family responsibilities. It was only in 1948, after the partition of the country, that I found the requisite leisure to indulge in extensive reading. This was during my stay in Bombay. I bought a number of books including *The Sacred Writings of the World's Great Religions, The Bible of the World* and a few other books, which explained in simple and concise language, the writings and essence of different religions. The books were written in simple English and they whetted my appetite for reading the principal texts of the great religions.

My first book, *Unity in Diversity*, with a foreword by Dr. Mulk Raj Anand, is a guide to the underlying principles of ethics and morals of the great religions of the world. The book created history in the publishing world and has already been brought out in thirteen Indian and foreign languages including German, French, Esperanto, and is now under production in twelve more foreign and Indian languages. It even has an edition in Braille which is being published by the Institute for the visually handicapped.

The book has been hailed as a positive contribution to the promotion of religious co-existence, national integration and international understanding. Encouraged by its success and the laudatory reviews it received from the press and comments from the public, I began working on a project of simplifying the scriptures.

Bhagavad Gita with a foreword by M.P. Pandit has been highly praised for its exposition, which has a simplicity and clarity of its own.

Japji with a foreword by Dr. Jaswant Singh Neki, has been widely appreciated for its clarification of complex expressions so that these become intelligible to the layman.

Selections from the Qur'an with a foreword by Prof. Rasheeduddin Khan, expounds on, the spirit and principles of Islam in understandable and simple English. It is meant specially for those who do not know Arabic, and their number runs into millions.

Selections from the Bible is the last volume of the project. The selections have been made from The New Testament, known as the authorized version, and rewritten in simple

English. They give the essence of Christian teachings.

I am sure the book will draw the reader to the study of the full text of the Bible.

O.P. Ghai

Acknowledgements

I express my deep act of gratitude to scholars of Christian religion, philosophy and history — too many to acknowledge individually — whose books I have consulted in the preparation of this work, while learning a lot from them.

I am thankful to Mrs. Vijaya Kumar, who has, with love and devotion, edited the manuscript with great care.

I am also thankful to Ms. Jaishree Rawat who prepared a flawless copy for the press.

Last but not least, I am most grateful to Reverend Father T.V. Kunnunkal for going through the manuscript and writing an excellent and inspiring foreword to the book. Besides, he gave me a few books with modern translations of the Bible which helped me while giving finishing touches to the manuscript.

O.P. Ghai

Shri O.P. Ghai (1919-1992) passed away peacefully on the morning of May 6, 1992. He handed over to me the complete manuscript of this book on May 4, 1992. It was his cherished dream to complete the project 'Simplifying the Scriptures'. He did so, but sadly did not live to see the last of his books on this project in print.

S.K. Ghai

Introduction

The New Testament is the sacred book of the Christians. Though it is referred to as a book, it is actually a collection of twenty-seven books or writings. These writings were chosen from the mass of religious literature which was circulated among the early Christians. These writings first appeared in the Greek language. They have since been translated into almost all the known languages of the world. Innumerable versions are available in English. Early in the 17th century, King James of England ordered the English translation which is known as the Authorisd Version of the Bible.

A few papyri fragments date back to the 2nd century, while full manuscripts of the New Testament date as far back as the 4th or the 5th century, while still others belong to a period, sometime between the 5th and 6th centuries. The oldest complete manuscript of the New Testament, *Codesc Sinaitieus*, is in London.

The Christian Messiah, Jesus of Nazareth, was a Jew, deeply steeped in Jewish tradition and culture. He was brought up according to the customs of the Jewish community. He knew the Law. He assured his followers that his mission was to interpret the deepest meaning of the Law, namely God's self-revelation to the Jewish people. He thought of himself as one in a line of Prophets to give a true interpretation to what was to be put into words and deeds.

Soon, Jesus and his followers developed differences from the narrow nationalism of Judaism. Having understood the significance of Jesus Christ, his disciples carried the high ethical idealism of the greatest of the Prophets to all people, both Jew and non-Jew; his gospel was for all.

The first four books of the New Testament, known as the Gospel according to Matthew, Mark, Luke and John respectively, account and interpret the life of Jesus.

The fifth book is the story of the followers of Jesus after he died. It tells about the founding of the Christian Church by a small band of his followers.

The next twenty-one books of the Testament are letters written by the early Christians, most of them by St. Paul, the foremost Christian missionary. He wrote letters to the churches which he founded and several other churches. The authorship of some of the other letters is not known.

The last book in the New Testament, Revelation, is an example of the mass of literature which was circulated among the churches. It is an account of a vision experienced by John and is written in symbolic language. There are many interpretations of this book.

Growing out of the teachings of Jesus of Nazareth, Christianity developed into a religious movement in and beyond the Roman Empire. The

Christians were at first persecuted by Jewish and Roman authorities but eventually Christianity became an official religion under Emperor Constantine. Gradually, it dominated Europe and the Middle East and spread throughout the world. Its missionary activities have carried it to all parts of the globe. The Bible has been translated into more than 1,000 languages. Christians today form the largest religious group in the world.

The Gospel according to Saint Matthew

This first book in the New Testament was probably written in Palestine between A.D. 70 and A.D. 80 and is attributed to one named Levi who was often called Matthew. It was probably written for Jewish Christians who were in conflict with their Jewish contemporaries. The events are grouped according to their similarity and not according to the strict chronological order. The book alternates between narrative and collections of teachings.

Chapter 3

Repent for the Kingdom of heaven is at hand.

Verse 2

Chapter 5

Blessed are the poor in spirit: the Kingdom of heaven is theirs.

Blessed are the sorrowful: they shall be comforted.

Blessed are the gentle: they shall inherit the earth.

Blessed are they who hunger and thirst for uprightness: they shall be satisfied.

Blessed are the merciful: they shall get mercy.

Blessed are the pure in heart: they shall see God.

Blessed are the peacemakers: they shall be called the children of God.

Blessed are those who are persecuted for the sake of uprightness: the Kingdom of heaven is theirs.

Blessed are you, when people abuse you and persecute you and say all manner of evil against you falsely, for my sake.

Rejoice, and be very glad: for you will have a great reward in heaven: they persecuted the prophets before you in the same way.

Verses 3-12

You are the light of the world. A city that stands on a hill cannot be hidden.

Men do not light a candle, and put it under a bowl; they put it on a candlestand; and it gives light to everyone in the house.

Shed light among your fellows, so that they may see your good works and praise your Father in heaven.

Do do think that I have come to destroy the law, or the prophets: I have not come to destroy, but to complete.

Verses 14-17

But let your communication be, 'yes', or 'no': for whatsoever is more than that, comes from the devil.

You have heard that it has been said, "An eye for an eye, and a tooth for a tooth."

But what I tell you is that you should not do wrong to a man who does you wrong:

Verses 37-39

If a man helps you to go one mile, go with him two.

Give to him who asks you, and do not turn away from the one who comes to borrow from you.

Verses 41-42

If you love only those who love you, what reward can you expect? Even the tax collectors do this.

If you greet your brothers only, you do not do anything extraordinary. Even the heathens do it.

Verses 46-47

Chapter 6

Do not boast about your religion before others; if you do, you will not be rewarded in your Father's house in heaven.

When you do some act of charity, do not publicly announce it as the hypocrites do in synagogues and in the streets to win people's admiration. You should know that they have their reward already.

When you give alms, let not your left hand know what your right hand does.

Do your good deeds in secret: your Father who sees what is done in secret will reward you openly.

And when you pray, you should not imitate the hypocrites who love to pray standing in the synagogues and in the corners of the streets, so that they are seen. Your Father knows what you need before you ask Him.

But when you pray, go into a room by yourself, shut the door and pray to your Father who is there in the secret place, and your Father who sees what is secret will reward you openly.

Verses 1-6

So pray like this: Our Father in heaven, may your name be held holy.
Your kingdom come. Your will, be done on earth as in heaven.
Give us today our daily bread.
And forgive us our sins, as we forgive those who sin against us.
And do not tempt us, but save us from the evil one.

Verses 9-13

No man can serve two masters; for either he will hate the first, and love the second; or he will be devoted to the first, and despise the second. You cannot serve both God and wealth.
I tell you not to worry about your life, your food and your drink. You should

not worry about your body and the clothes to cover it. Life is surely more than food, and the body more than clothes.

Verse 25

Look at the birds in the sky: they do not sow or reap or store in barns; yet your heavenly Father feeds them. Are you not worth more than the birds? Do not be anxious about tomorrow: tomorrow will take care of itself. Each day has enough troubles of its own.

Verse 34

Chapter 7

Do not judge, and you will not be judged.

As you judge others, so will you be judged: the same yardstick to judge you will be used to judge others.

Why do you observe the small piece of wood in your brother's eye and never notice the log in your own?

Verses 1-3

Always treat others as you would like them to treat you: that is the law and the prophecy.

Verse 12

Chapter 8

Jesus said, "The foxes have holes, and the birds of the air have nests; but the Son of man has nowhere to lay his head."

Chapter 9

While Jesus sat at the table in the house, many tax-collectors and sinners sat down with him and his disciples.

The Pharisees saw this and said to his disciples, "Why does your master eat with tax-collectors and sinners?"

Jesus heard this and replied, "It is not the healthy but the sick who need the doctor."

"Go and learn the meaning of the words. What pleases me is mercy and not sacrifice: for I have come to call the sinners and not the upright."

Verses 10-13

No one sews a piece of unshrinkable cloth on to an old cloak; because the piece pulls away from the cloak, leaving a bigger hole.

Nor do people put new wine into the old wine skins. If they do, the wine skins burst and the wine runs out and the skins perish: They put new wine into fresh skins, and both are preserved.

Verses 16-17

Then he touched their eyes, saying, "As you have believed, so let it be," and their sight was restored.

Verse 29

Chapter 10

Heal the sick, cleanse the lepers, raise the dead, cast out devils. You have received without making any payment; so give without charging anything.

Verse 8

Look, I am sending you out like sheep among wolves; so be wise as serpents, and harmless as doves.

Verse 16

The disciples is not superior to his teacher, nor is the servant above his master.

Verse 24

So do not be afraid of them; for everything covered shall be revealed, and everything hidden will be made known.

Verse 26

Do not be afraid of those who kill the body, but cannot kill the soul: yet fear him who can destroy both the soul and the body in hell.

Verse 28

Chapter 11

Anyone who has ears, should listen.

Verse 15

All of you who labour and are overburdened, come to me, and I will give you rest.

Take my yoke upon you and learn of me; for I am gentle and humble in heart: and you will find rest for your souls.

For my yoke is easy, and my burden is light.

Verses 28-30

Chapter 12

Jesus knew their thoughts and said to them, "Every kingdom divided against itself is heading for ruin; and every city or house divided against itself cannot stand."

Verse 25

Anyone who does the will of my Father in heaven, is my brother, and sister, and mother.

Verse 50

Chapter 13

Anyone who has something to give, will be given more, and will have more than enough: but anyone who has nothing to give, will be deprived of even what he has.

Therefore I speak to them in parables: because they who look without seeing, and listen without hearing, they do not understand.

Verses 12-13

They were offended by what he had said. This led Jesus to say, "A prophet is always held in honour, except in his own country, and in his own family."

Verse 57

Chapter 15

He called the people and said, "Listen to me, and understand.

'A man is not defiled by what goes into his mouth, but what comes out of it."

Verses 10-11

Let them alone: they are blind leaders of the blind. And if one blind leads another, both will fall into the ditch.

Verse 14

Chapter 16

Anyone who wants to save his life will lose it; but anyone who loses his life for my sake will find it.

What will a man gain if by winning the whole world he loses his own soul? Or what can a man give to get back his soul?

Verses 25-26

Chapter 18

I assure you that unless you change and become innocent like little children, you will never enter the kingdom of heaven.

The greatest in the kingdom of heaven is one who humbles himself and becomes like the child.

And whoever welcomes one such child in my name, welcomes me.

If anyone causes one of these little ones to lose his faith in me, it will be better for him to have a large millstone tied around his neck, and be drowned in the depths of the sea.

It is terrible for the world that certain offences are committed for such offences will happen, but how terrible for the man who causes them.

If your hand or your foot is the cause of your losing faith, cut them and throw them away: it is better for you to enter into life without a hand or a foot rather than having two hands or two feet and be thrown into the eternal fire.

And if your eye makes you lose your faith, pluck it out and throw it away: it is better for you to enter into life with only one eye rather than have two eyes and be thrown into the fire of hell.

Verses 3-9

Wherever, two or three come together in my name, I am there among them.

Verse 20

Chapter 19

They are no longer two but one. What God has joined together must not be separated by man. (*On marriage*)

Verse 6

Jesus said to them, "Let the children come to me, do not try to stop them: for the kingdom of heaven belongs to such as these." 40

Honour your father and your mother: and love your neighbour as yourself.

Verse 19

Jesus looked at them and said, "For men this is impossible, but everything is possible for God."

Verse 26

Chapter 20

"Why are you wasting the whole day here doing nothing?" he asked them. They answered, "Because no one hired us." He said to them, "Go and work in the vineyard, and whatever is rightly yours you will receive."

Verses 6-7

Jesus said, "So those who are last will be first, and those who are first will be last."

Verse 16

If one of you wants to be great, he must be your minister.

If any one of you wants to be chief, he must be your slave.

Even the Son of man came not to be served, but to serve and give his life to redeem many people.

Verses 26-28

Chapter 21

They said to Jesus, "Do you hear what they are saying?" And Jesus replied, "Yes, I do. Have you never ever read this scripture? You have trained children and babies to offer perfect praise."

Verse 16

If you believe, you will receive whatever you ask for in prayer.

Verse 22

Chapter 22

Jesus said, "Many are invited, but few are chosen."

Verse 14

So Jesus said to them. "Pay the emperor what belongs to the emperor, and pay God what belongs to God."

Verse 21

Chapter 23

The greatest one among you must be your servant.

Whosoever exalts himself will be humbled; and whosoever humbles himself will be exalted.

Verses 11-12

Blind Pharisee: Cleanse first the inside of the cup, then the outside will be clean also.

Verse 26

Chapter 24

Wherever there is a dead body, the vultures will gather.

Verse 28

Chapter 25

The master said to him, "Well done, you good and trustworthy servant: you have been trustworthy in small things; I will now trust you for bigger things. Come and share your master's happiness."

Verse 21

For when I was hungry you gave me food: when I was thirsty you gave me drink, and when I was a stranger, you welcomed me into your home.

When I was naked you clothed me: when I was sick, you visited me: and when I was in prison, you came to see me.

Verses 35-36

The king will reply: "I tell you, whatever you have done for one of my brothers, you have done for me."

Verse 40

Chapter 26

You will always have the poor among you; but you will not have me always. Keep awake and pray, that you will not fall into temptation: the spirit is willing but the flesh is weak.

Verse 41

Chapter 27

Jesus gave a loud cry and breathed his last.

Verse 50

The curtain hanging in the temple was torn in two from top to bottom; there was an earthquake and the rocks split apart.

Verse 52

The graves opened and many saints rose from sleep.

Verse 52

Chapter 28

Teach them to obey everything I have commanded: and I will be with you always, even to the end of time.

Verse 20

The Gospel according to Saint Mark

This gospel is attributed to Mark between A.D. 60 and 70. Early tradition says that he was a close friend of St. Peter and seems to have got most of his material from Peter. The gospel was written, it is believed, in Rome and for the Gentile Christians of that city. The major themes are the cost of discipleship and the meaning of what Jesus, who was finally crucified, taught.

Chapter 2

And Jesus said to them, "The Sabbath was made for the good of man; man was not made for the Sabbath."

Verse 27

Chapter 4

There is nothing hidden, which will not be disclosed and what is covered will come into the open.

Verse 22

Chapter 9

For everyone will be salted with fire, and every sacrifice will be salted.

Salt is good; but if it loses its saltiness, what will you season with? Have salt in yourselves and be at peace with one another.

Verses 49-50

Chapter 10

Some people brought their children to Jesus for him to touch them: and his disciples scolded them.

When Jesus saw this, he was very unhappy, and said to them, "Let the little children come to me, and do not stop them: because the Kingdom of God belongs to them."

Verses 13-14

Chapter 11

I tell you: when you pray and ask for something, believe that you have received it, and it will be yours.

And when you stand and pray, forgive whatever you have against anyone, so that your Father in heaven may forgive you the wrongs you have done.

Verses 24-25

Chapter 12

And have you not read this scripture: the stone which the builders rejected has become the most important of all.

Verse 10

Chapter 13

Everyone will hate you because of me: but the man who holds out to the end will be saved.

Verse 13

Chapter 16

Then he said to them, "Go to every part of the world, and preach the gospel to all mankind."

Verse 15

The Gospel according to Saint Luke

The author of this gospel was called Luke, short for Lucanus. He was a Gentile and a physician, who was very close to St. Paul, being with him both the times when imprisoned by the Romans. Scholars are of the opinion that the gospel was written between A.D. 70 and A.D. 80. It seeks to show Jesus as the saviour of the human race and that he was a prophet who was specially committed to the poor sinners, the outcastes of the society and women, and whose teachings are very challenging. Special emphasis is given to the infancy of Jesus and his appearance to his disciples after his death.

Chapter 1

Mary said:

My soul proclaims the greatness of the Lord

My spirit is glad because of God, my Saviour.

For He has remembered me, His lowly servant.

From now on all people will call me blessed.

Because He the Mighty God has done great things for me: and His name is Holy.

He shows mercy to those who honour Him from generation to generation.

He has shown the strength of His mighty arm; He has scattered the proud with all their plans.

He has filled the hungry with good things; and has sent away the rich empty handed.

He has kept the promise He made to our ancestors and has come to help His servant Israel. He has remembered to show mercy to Abraham and to all His descendants forever.

Verses 46-55

Let us praise the God of Israel: for He has turned to His people, saved them and set them free.

He has provided for us a mighty Saviour, a descendant of His servant David.

He promised through His holy prophets long ago:

That He would save us from our enemies, and from all those who hate us;

That He would show mercy to our fathers, and remember His sacred covenant;

Such was the oath which He swore to our father Abraham.

He promised to rescue us from our enemies and allow us to serve Him without fear,

And worship Him with uprightness of heart, all the days of our life.

And you, my child, will be called the prophet of the Highest: for you will go ahead of the Lord to prepare His ways;

To lead the people to salvation through knowledge of Him, by the forgiveness of their sins.

Through the tender mercy of our God; the morning sun from heaven will rise upon us;

And shine on those who live in dark shadow of death, to guide our steps into the path of peace.

Verses 68-79

Chapter 3

Someone is shouting in the desert:

Prepare the way for the Lord, clear a straight path for him.

Every valley must be filled up and every hill and mountain levelled off; the winding roads must be made straight, and the rough paths made smooth, for all mankind will see God's salvation!

Verses 4-6

Then prove your repentance by doing good deeds and do not begin saying amongst yourselves, we have Abraham for our father. I tell you that

God can make children for Abraham out of the stones.

Verse 8

Chapter 4

The spirit of the Lord is upon me, because he has chosen me to bring good news to the poor; he has sent me to heal the broken-hearted, to proclaim liberty to the captives and recovery of sight to the blind; and to set at liberty the oppressed.

Verses 18-19

And announce that the time has come when the Lord will save his people.

And he said to them, "I am sure that you will quote this proverb, 'Physician, heal yourself,' and say we have heard of what you did in

Capernaum, do the same here in our home town."

Verse 23

Chapter 6

Happy are you who are hungry now: you will be filled! Happy are you who weep now; you will laugh!

Verse 21

Give to everyone who asks you; when a man takes away what is your, do not ask for it back.

If you do good only to those who do good to you, it gives you no credit. Even sinners do as much.

And if you lend only to those from whom you hope to receive it back, why should you be thanked? Even sinners lend to each other to be repaid in full. *Verses 33-34*

Give to others and God will give to you; indeed, you will receive a generous helping, as much as your can hold. The measure you use for others is the same that God will use for you.

Verse 38

Chapter 7

I tell you, her sins which are many, have been forgiven; because she has shown much love: but for whom little is forgiven, they love only a little.

Verse 47

Chapter 8

Everything that is hidden will be made public; and whatever is covered up will be found and brought to light.

Verse 17

Chapter 9

And he said to them all, "If any one wants to be my follower, he must forget self, take up his cross everyday and come with me."

Verse 23

Jesus said to him, "Do not stop him: because whoever is not against you is with you."

Verse 50

Jesus said to him, "No one, who looks back, once having put his hand to the plough, is fit for the Kingdom of God."

Verse 62

Chapter 10

Whichever house you enter, let your first words be, "Peace be to this house."

Verse 5

Stay in the same house, eating and drinking whatever they offer you: for a worker should be given his due. Do not move from house to house.

Verse 7

Chapter 11

I say to you, "Ask and you will receive; seek, and you will find; knock, and the door will be opened to you."

For everyone who asks will receive; and he who seeks will find, and the door will be opened to anyone who knocks.

Verses 9-10

He who is not with me is against me: and he who does not gather with me, is really scattering.

Verse 23

Give in charity whatever you have; and everything is clean for you.

Verse 41

Chapter 12

Are not five sparrows sold for two pennies? Yet not one of them is forgotten by God.

Verse 6

Can anyone of you, by worrying over it, live a bit longer?

Verse 25

Look how the wild flowers grow: they do not work, or make clothes for themselves; and yet I tell you that even King Solomon with all his wealth did not have clothes as beautiful as one of these flowers.

Sell whatever you have, and give in charity; provide for yourselves purses that do not wear out, and save your riches in heaven, where they will never decrease, because no thief can get to them, and no moth can destroy them.

Verse 33

Gird up your loins, and be ready for action with your lights lit.

Verse 35

I have come to set fire to the earth; and how I wish it were already kindled.

Verse 49

Do you suppose that I have come to bring peace to the world? No, not peace, but division.

Verses 51

Chapter 14

When you give a feast, invite the poor, the maimed, the lame and the blind;

And you will be blessed; for they are not able to pay you back: God will repay you on the day the good people rise from death.

Verses 13-14

Whoever comes to me cannot be my disciple unless he loves me more than his father, his mother, his wife and his children, his brothers and his sisters, and himself as well.

Verse 26

Chapter 15

I tell you, that there will be more joy in heaven over one sinner who repents than over ninety-nine just persons who do not need to repent.

Verse 7

Chapter 16

It is easier for heaven and earth to come to an end, than for the smallest detail of the Law to be removed.

Verse 17

Chapter 17

Keep watch over yourself! If your brother wrongs you, rebuke him; and it he repents, forgive him.

If he wrongs you seven times in a day, and comes back to you each time, saying, "I am sorry," you must forgive him.

Verses 3-4

No one will say, "Look, here it is!" or, "There it is!" because the Kingdom of God is within you.

Verse 21

Chapter 18

It is easier for a camel to go through the eye of a needle than for a rich man to enter the Kingdom of God.

Verse 25

Jesus said, "I tell you, that there is no man who has given up his home or parents or brothers or wife or children, for the sake of the kingdom of God.

Such men will be better rewarded in this present age, and in the eternal life in the age to come."

Verses 29-30

Chapter 19

He said to the servant, "I will judge you by your own words. You know that I am a hard man, that I take what is not mine, draw out what I never put in."

Verse 22

Chapter 21

By standing firm, you will save yourself.

Verse 19

Heaven and earth will pass away, but my words will forever remain.

Verse 33

Chapter 23

For if such things as these are done when the wood is green, what will happen when it is dry?

Verse 31

Then Jesus gave a loud cry and said, "Father! Into your hands I commit my spirit!" and saying this he died.

Verse 46

Chapter 24

He is not here; he has been raised. Remember what he said to you while he was in Galilee.

Verse 6

The Gospel according to Saint John

This gospel has been called 'the most influential book in all literature'. Scholars agree that St. John, the apostle of Jesus, had a profound influence on this gospel which was completed probably between A.D. 80 and A.D. 95. He omits much that is found in the other gospels, but has included many discourses of Jesus and discussions on controversial points. Further, the Jesus of this gospel is a mystical individual of deep spiritual understanding.

This gospel has distinctive characteristics and contains incidents and teachings not found in the other gospels.

Chapter 1

Light shines brighter in the darkness; and darkness has never put it out.

Verse 5

Chapter 2

He made a whip from the small cords and drove all the animals, the sheep and the oxen out of the temple; he overthrew the tables of the money-changers and scattered their coins.

He ordered the men who sold the pigeons, "Take these things and do not make my Father's house a market place."

Verses 15-16

Chapter 3

The wind blows where it wishes; you hear the sound it makes, but cannot tell where it comes from and where it is going. It is like that with everyone who is born of the Spirit.

Verse 8

Chapter 4

You Samaritans worship but do not really know whom: but we Jews know whom we worship, because it is from the Jews that salvation comes.

Verse 22

God is a spirit: and only by the power of his Spirit can people worship him as he really is.

Verse 24

The saying is true, "One man sows, another man reaps."

Verse 37

Chapter 5

He answered, "The man who made me well, told me to pick up my mat and walk."

 Verse 11

Chapter 6

Jesus told them, "I am the bread of life. He who comes to me will never be hungry; and he who believes in me will never be thirsty."

Verse 35

Everyone whom my Father gives me will come to me; I will not turn away anyone who comes to me.

Verse 37

I am telling you the truth, He who believes in me has eternal life.

Verse 47

Chapter 8

As they continued asking him questions he straightened himself up and said to them, "He who is without sin among you may throw the first stone on her."

Verse 7

Jesus spoke to the Pharisees again and told them, "I am the light of the world: he who follows me will have the light of life and will never walk in darkness."

Verse 12

Chapter 11

Jesus said to her, "I am the resurrection and the life: he who believes in me will live, even though he dies.

He who lives and believes in me will never die. Do you believe this?"

Verses 25-26

Chapter 12

I am telling you the truth, a grain of wheat remains no more a single grain until it falls on the ground and dies. But if it dies it bears a rich harvest.

Verses 24-25

Jesus said to them, "The light will be with you for a little longer. Continue on your way while you have the light, so that the darkness will not come upon you: he who walks in the darkness does not know where he is going."

Verse 35

Chapter 13

I am not talking about all of you: I know those I have chosen. But the scripture must come true that says, "The man who shared my food turned against me."

Verse 18

And now I give you a new commandment: love one another. As I have loved you, you must love one another.

If you have love for one another everyone will know that you are my disciple.

Verses 34-35

Jesus told them, "Do not be worried and upset. Believe in God and believe also in me."

There are many rooms in my Father's house; I would not tell you this if it were not so. I am going to prepare a place for you.

Verses 1-2

Thomas said to him, "Lord we do not know where you are going; so how can we know the way to get there?"

Verse 5

Jesus answered, "I have been with you all for a long time; yet you do not know me, Philip? Whoever has seen

73

me has seen the Father. Why, then do you say, "Show us the Father?"

Verse 9

Believe me when I say that I am in the Father, and the Father is in me. If you do not believe this, believe because of the things I do.

Verse 11

If you ask me for anything in my name I will do it.

If you love me, you will obey my commandments.

I will ask the Father, and he will give you another helper, who will stay with you for ever.

Verses 14-16

When I go you will not be all alone; I will come back to you.

Verse 18

Jesus answered and said to him, "Whosoever loves me, will obey my teachings: and my Father will love him, and we will come to him and live with him.

Whosoever does not love me will not obey my teaching: and the teaching you have heard is not mine but comes from the Father who sent me.

Verses 23-24

Peace is what I leave with you: it is my own peace that I give you not as the world does. Do not be worried and upset, nor be afraid.

Verse 27

Chapter 15

Remain united to me and I will remain united to you. A branch cannot bear fruit by itself, it can do so only if it remains in the vine; similarly, you cannot bear fruit unless you remain in me.

I am the wine, you are the branches: whosoever remains in me and I in him, will bear much fruits: for without me you can do nothing.

Verses 4-5

The greatest love a person can have for his friends is to lay down his life for them.

Verse 13

Chapter 16

So far I have been using figures of speech to tell you these things: the time will come when I will not use figures of speech but will speak to you plainly about the Father.

Verse 25

I have told you all this, so that you may find peace in me. In the world you will have trouble: be cheerful, I have conquered the world!

Verse 33

The Acts of the Apostles

This book, usually referred to as 'Acts', was written by 'Luke', the author of the third gospel, sometime between A.D. 62 and A.D. 70.

The material in the first part of the book is based on the research of Luke, as he talked with others. However, the latter parts of the book are written from first-hand experiences since he was a close friend and companion of St. Paul.

Since Luke considered this book as a continuation of his other books, the Gospel, he gave it no title.

Chapter 3

Then Peter said to him, "I have no money at all; but I give you whatever little I have. In the name of Jesus Christ of Nazareth I order you to get up and walk."

Verse 6

Chapter 10

He started at him in fear, and the angel said, "What is it, my Lord?" The angel said, "Your prayers and your acts of charity have gone up to heaven to speak for you before God."

Verse 4

Peter said, "I now realize that God treats everyone alike."

In every nation the man who is God-fearing and does what is right is acceptable to him.

Verses 34-35

Chapter 17

God who made the world and everything in it, is Lord of Heaven and Earth and does not live in man-made temples.

Verse 24

From one man he created all races of mankind and made them live throughout the whole earth. He himself determined beforehand the exact times and the limits of their territory.

Verse 26

In him, we live and move and exist; some of your own poets have said, "We are also his offspring."

Verse 28

I have shown you in all things that by working hard thus, we should help the weak, we should remember the words of Lord Jesus, who himself said, "Happiness lies more in giving than in receiving.

Verse 35

The Epistle to the Romans

This is a letter that St. Paul wrote to the Roman Church of the Greek speaking population, which comprised both Jews and Gentiles, many of whom had migrated to Rome while others were natives of that city. It was written in Corinth, in the Greek language, during the spring of A.D. 58. Paul recognized the importance of the church in Rome, the capital of a great empire, and devoted much thought to this letter in order to impress upon the members the importance of unity in faith and fidelity to their faith, explaining his interpretation of Jesus's teaching showing the relationship between the Jewish religion and the Law.

Chapter 1

The Gospel reveals God's way of righting the wrong. It is through having faith from the beginning to the end. The scripture says, "He, who through faith, is put right with God, will live."

Verse 17

Chapter 2

You have no excuse at all; you, who sit in judgement, whoever you may be be: you condemn yourself when you judge others and then do the same things which they do.

We know that God is right when He judges the people who do such things as these.

Verses 1-2

God will reward every person according to what he has done.

Verse 6

God judges everyone with the same standard.

Verse 11

Chapter 5

We also boast of our troubles because we know that trouble produces endurance.

Endurance brings God's approval and his approval creates hopes.

Verses 3-4

As by the disobedience of one man, many were made sinners, so by the obedience of one man many will be made righteous.

The law entered into the process to multiply law breaking. But when sin increased, God's grace increased much more.

Verse 20

Chapter 6

The wages of sin is death; but God's gift is eternal life in union with Jesus Christ our Lord.

Verse 23

Chapter 7

The good which I want to do I fail to do: what I do is the wrong which I do not want to do.

Verse 19

Chapter 8

What the law could not do, because human nature was weak, God did. He condemned sin in human nature by sending his own Son, who came with a nature like man's sinful nature, to do away with sin.

Verse 3

Those who live as their human nature tells them to, have their minds controlled by what human nature wants. Those who live as the Spirit tells them to live, have their minds controlled by what the Spirit wants.

To be controlled by human nature, results in death; to be controlled by the Spirit results in life and peace.

Verses 5-6

You do not live as your human nature tells you to; instead you live as the spirit tells you to live, if God's spirit lives in you. If a man does not possess the Spirit of Christ, he is no Christian.

Verse 9

If you live according to your human nature, you will die: but if by Spirit you put your sinful action to death, you will live.

Verse 13

Creation itself would one day be set free from its slavery to decay and would share the glorious freedom of the children of God.

Verse 21

We know that in all things God works for good of those who love him, those whom he has called according to his purpose.

Verse 28

Who, then, can separate us from the love of Christ? Can trouble do it, or hardship or persecution or hunger or poverty or danger or death?

Verse 35

Chapter 9

After all the potter can do what he likes with his clay; is he not free to make two vessels out of the same lump, one to be treasured and the other for common use?

Verse 21

Chapter 12

Have the same concern for others as you have for yourself. Do not be proud, but be humble with common folk. Do not think of yourselves as wise.

Never pay back evil for evil. Try to do what everyone considers to be good.

Verses 16-17

Do not let evil conquer you, but overcome evil with good.

Verses 21

Chapter 13

Do not be under obligation to anyone, only love one another! Whosoever does this has obeyed the law.

Do not commit adultery, do not commit murder, do not steal, do not bear false witness, do not envy; for all these, and many others besides, are summed up in the one command, "Love your neighbour as you love yourself."

Verses 8-9

The night is nearly over, the day is almost here: let us stop doing things that belong to the dark and let us take up weapons for fighting in the light.

Verse 12

Chapter 14

None of us lives for himself only, and none of us dies for himself only.

Verse 17

As a Christian I am absolutely convinced that there is nothing impure in itself: if a man considers anything impure then to him it becomes impure.

Verse 14

It is good to abstain from eating meat, or drinking wine, or doing anything which causes your brothers' downfall. Have you faith? Have it to yourself, than between yourself and God. Happy is he who can make his decision with a clear conscience.

Even if he has doubts about his food, God condemns him when he eats it, because his action is not based on faith.

And anything that is not based on faith is sin.

*Verses 21-23*

Chapter 15

We who are strong in the faith ought to help the weak to carry their burdens, and not to please ourselves.

Verse 1

All the ancient scriptures were written for our instruction, so that through the encouragement they give us, we may maintain our hope with fortitude.

Verse 4

The First Epistle to the Corinthians

This letter was written to the church at Corinth by St. Paul, probably around A.D. 57. At this time Paul was in Ephesus, stopping there on his third great missionary journey. This church was located in the centre of a city that had become the commercial and political capital of Greece. Because of the background of the believers, they misunderstood some aspects of Christian life and Paul wrote seeking to admonish the members for their sins and divisions and to restore them to the purity of Christian life.

Chapter 1

In order to shame the wise, God chose what the world considered foolish; he chose what the world considers weak, to put to shame the strong.

Verse 27

Chapter 3

The work of each man will at last be brought to light: it will be exposed on the day of judgement; on that day, fire will reveal everyone's work; the fire will test and show its real quality.

If the work survives, the builder will receive a reward.

Verses 13-14

Chapter 7

To the unmarried and the widows, I say that it would be better for them to continue to live alone.

But if you cannot control your desires, it will be better to marry, than to burn with passion.

Verses 8-9

God bought you for a price; so do not become slaves of man.

Verse 23

Chapter 8

But the person who loves God is known to him.

Verse 3

There is for us only one God, the Father, who is a Creator of all things, and for whom we live; and there is only one Lord, Jesus Christ, through whom all things were created and through whom we live.

Verse 6

Chapter 9

We read in the law of Moses. "Do not muzzle on ox when you are using it to thresh corn." Do you think that God is concerned about oxen?

Is the reference clearly to ourselves? Of course, it refers to us, in the sense that the plougher should plough and the thresher thresh in the hope of getting some of the produce.

Verses 9-10

Do you not know that at the sports all the runners run the race though only one wins the prize? Run, then, in such a way that you win the prize.

Verse 24

Chapter 10

Whosoever thinks that he standing firm should be careful that he does not fall.

Verse 12

Whether you eat, or drink, or whatever you do, do it all for God's glory.

Verse 31

Chapter 12

Just as a body is one, even if it has many parts, so is Christ who has many parts but still one body.

Verse 12

Chapter 13

Love is patient, and kind; and envies no one; love is not conceited, or proud.

Verse 4

Chapter 14

There are many different languages in the world, yet none of them is without meaning.

Verse 10

Chapter 15

If, as the saying goes, I have fought with wild beasts in Ephesus, what have I gained by it? If the dead are never raised to life, "Let us eat and drink, for tomorrow we die."

Do not be fooled: bad companions ruin good character.

Verses 32-33

You fool! When you sow a seed in the ground, it does not sprout to life unless it dies.

Verse 36

Chapter 16

Be alert, stand firm in the faith, be brave, be strong.

Do all your work in love.

Verses 13-14

The Second Epistle
to the Corinthians

St. Paul's first letter to the church at Corinth was not well received. His relations with the Corinthian church during a visit were painful, his failure to make a later visit, and the activities of the opponents created real tensions between Paul and this community. St. Paul's opponents used all means possible to dispute his teachings and break up the Corinthian church. So in A.D. 55-56, Paul wrote another letter to the church in which he sought to justify himself and his work. For this reason, the letter is autobiographical and is largely a defence of Paul's acts and an exposition of his faith.

Chapter 5

Our life is a matter of faith, not of sight.

Verse 7

Chapter 6

God says, "When the time came for me to show you favour, I heard you: when the day arrived for me to save you I helped you." The hour of faith has come now; the day of deliverance has dawned.

Verse 2

Although saddened, we are always glad; we seem poor but we make many people rich; we seem to have nothing, yet we really possess everything.

Verse 10

Chapter 8

As the Scripture says, "The one who gathered much did not have too much, and the one who gathered little did not have too little."

Verse 15

Chapter 9

Each one should give as he has decided, not with regret or out of a sense of duty; for God loves one who gives gladly.

Verse 7

Chapter 10

We do not war according to the flesh even though we walk in the flesh, For our weapons are not carnal but the mighty in God.

Verses 3-4

The weapons we use in our fight are not the world's weapons, but God's powerful weapons to demolish strongholds.

Verse 4

Chapter 11

I know how happy you are to put up with fools, being so wise yourself.

Verse 19

Chapter 12

His answer was, "My grace is all you need, for my power is greatest when you are weak." I am most happy, then, to be proud of my weaknesses in order to feel the protection of Christ's power over me.

Verse 9

This is now the third time that I am ready to come to visit you and I will not make any demands on you. It is you I want, not your money. After all, children should not have to provide for their parents, but parents should provide for their children.

Verse 14

The Epistle to the Galatians

It is not certain whether St. Paul wrote this letter (in A.D. 54-55) only to the churches in Galatia proper or to those in the whole Roman province of Galatia, a much larger territory. But, in either case, the Galatian churches were highly fickle. While Paul was with them, they had accepted his preaching with enthusiasm. But later the Judaizers' argument that they had to obey the Jewish laws in order to be good Christians nearly convinced them. To counter such teaching, Paul wrote this letter. In the letter, written with great emotion, Paul seeks to show that Jesus had freed men from the bondage of the ancient Mosaic law.

Chapter 5

It takes a little yeast to make the whole lump of dough rise.

Verse 9

The law is summed up in one commandment, "Love your neighbour as you love yourself."

Verse 14

What our human nature wants is against what our Spirit wants, they are contrary to each other. This means that you cannot do what you want to do.

Verse 17

Chapter 6

Help to carry each others burdens and in this way you will obey the law of Christ.

Verse 2

Everyone has to carry his own load.

Verse 5

Do not deceive yourself; no one makes a fool of God: a person reaps exactly what he sows.

Verse 7

Let us not get tired of doing good; if we do not give up, the time will come when we will reap the harvest.

Verse 9

The Epistle to the Ephesians

This is possibly a circular letter which St. Paul or one of his companions sent to many of the churches. It was written possibly while he was a prisoner in Rome, about the year A.D. 63.

Here the emphasis is upon the catholicity of the church as the continuation of the spirit and energy of Jesus. This copy went to Ephesus, while other copies were sent to each of the churches in Asia.

Chapter 4

There is one body, and one Spirit, just as there is one hope to which God has called you.

There is one Lord, one faith, one baptism.

There is one God and Father of all mankind, who is Lord of all, works through all, and is in all.

Verses 4-6

If you become angry, do not let your anger lead you into sin, and do not stay angry all day.

Verse 26

Chapter 6

Put on all the armour that God gives you, so that you may be able to stand against the devil's evil.

We are not fighting against human beings but against authorities, cosmic powers of this dark age and against the super human forces of evil in the universe.

Therefore put on God's armour! Then you will be able to stand strong when things are at their worst, and after completing every task, you will still stand firm.

So stand ready, gird up your loins with truth, and do everything with integrity.

Let the shoes on your feet be the gospel of peace to give you firm footing.

At all times take up the great shield of faith; with it you will be able to quench the flaming arrows of the evil.

Accept salvation as a helmet, and the word of God as the sword which the Spirit gives you.

Verses 11-17

The Epistle to the Philippians

The church in Philippi was the one closest to the heart of St. Paul. He had visited it several times and had received pecuniary help from it. Among its members were many of his closest friends. Hence this letter is a spontaneous outflowing of his affection and regard for the church and his many close friends there. These friends were especially remembered at this time because they had sent him some help as he waited in a prison, probably in Ephasus, about A.D. 55-66. This is the only letter of Paul's in which there is no strong expression of rebuke or disappointment.

Chapter 4

And the peace of God, which is far beyond human understanding will keep your hearts and minds safe in union with Jesus Christ.

Finally, my brothers, fill your minds with those things which are true, pure, lovely, and honourable, and with those things in which there is virtue, and these deserve praise.

Verses 7-8

I am not saying this because I feel neglected, for I have learnt to be satisfied with what I have.

I know what it is to be in need and what it is to have more than enough. I have learnt this secret, so that anywhere, and at any time, I am content, whether I am full or hungry, whether I have too much or too little.

Verses 11-12

The Epistle to the Colossians

This letter was written to the church at Colossae, a town in Asia Minor, east of Ephesus. Paul had not established this church, but it was in an area for which he felt responsible as he sent out workers from Ephesus. He had learnt that there were false teachers in the church who insisted that one must worship certain 'spiritual rulers and authorities' in order to know God and have full salvation.

Paul wrote to oppose the teachings with the true Christian message, that Jesus Christ would lead them to salvation.

Chapter 2

Why do you let people dictate to you like - 'do not touch this', 'do not taste that' and 'do not handle the other'?

All these refer to things that become useless once they are used; they are only man-made rules and teachings.

Verses 21-22

Chapter 3

Set your thoughts on higher realms, and not to this earthily life.

Verse 2

Whatever you do, put your heart into it, as though you were working for the Lord, and not for men.

Verse 23

Chapter 4

Your conversation should always be gracious and interesting, and you should know how to answer each person.

Verse 6

The First Epistle to the Thessalonians

Probably it is the first of the letters of St. Paul, written late in A.D. 52 or early in A.D. 53 from Corinth. As such, it is believed to be the earliest Christian document now in existence. The church at Thessaloniaca was founded by Paul in A.D. 50 among the Jews who had moved to that city. But persecution was so severe that Paul had to flee the city. After he left, the church was affected by popular antagonism and propaganda against Paul. They misunderstood some of his teachings about the end of the world. Paul wrote to answer their questions and to admonish them for their sins.

Chapter 4

You should lead a quiet life, mind your own business, and earn your own living, as we told you before.

Verse 11

Chapter 5

Always be joyful.

Pray at all times.

Be thankful in all circumstances. This is what God wants from you in your life in union with Jesus Christ.

Verses 16-18

Put all things to the test; keep what is good.

Avoid all evil.

May the God who gives us peace make you holy in every way and keep your whole being spirit, soul, and body free from every fault at the coming of our Lord Jesus Christ.

Verses 21-23

The Second Epistle to the Thessalonians

This epistle was written probably by St. Paul sometime after the early part of A.D. 53 and before A.D. 58, possibly while he was still at Corinth from where he wrote the first epistle to the Thessalonians. In it Paul seeks to explain that the end of the world is not to be expected immediately and people should not become idle waiting for it. He urges that the members of the church continue to work and pray, as this is the best preparation for any end that may come.

Chapter 3

While we were with you, we used to say to you, "Whoever refuses to work is not allowed to eat."

Verse 10

The First Epistle to Timothy

Timothy a young Christian from Asia Minor, was the son of a Jewish mother and a Greek father. He became a companion and assistant to Paul in his missionary work. The letter deals with three specific points. The first is a warning against false teaching in the church. The second contains instructions about church administration and worship, with a description of the kind of character that church leaders should have. The third is advise to Timothy to be a good servant of Jesus Christ and his responsibilities towards various groups of believers.

Chapter 6

We brought nothing into this world, and it is certain that we can take nothing out.

Verse 7

The love of money is the root cause of all evil. Some have been so eager to have it that they have wandered away from the faith and have broken their hearts with many sorrows.

Verse 10

Do your best to run the great race of faith, and win eternal life for yourself; it was for this life that God called you when you firmly professed your faith before many witnesses.

Verse 12

The Second Epistle to Timothy

St. Paul wrote this letter to Timothy from his prison in Rome in either A.D. 67 or A.D. 68. When he wrote it, he was certain that death was near and he wanted very much to see his dear friend and aide. The letter is full of instructions to Timothy regarding the Christian way of life and work in the church. As such it has served as a manual of instructions to all ministers of the church.

Chapter 3

All Scriptures are inspired by God and are useful for teaching the truth, rebuking error, correcting faults, and in disciplining right living.

This will make the person serve God, fully qualified and equipped to do every kind of good deed.

Verses 16-17

The Epistle to Titus

This epistle was written by St. Paul to Titus, one of his most trusted apostles. Titus was an occasional companion of Paul, who seems to have worked more or less independently, but is known to have strong and stable faith in God. Paul wrote to him in about A.D. 65 to give him instructions for carrying on in Crete, the work that he had left incomplete. Thus, the letter has many direct and particular suggestions and directions for organising a regular ministry by appointing elders, and for combating false doctrines.

Chapter 1

All things are pure to those who are themselves pure; but nothing is pure to the tainted minds of disbelievers, for their minds and consciences have been defiled.

Verse 15

The Epistle to Philemon

Philemon was a prominent Christian, probably a member of the church at Colossae. He was the owner of a slave named Onesimus who ran away from him, and somehow had come in contact with Paul, who was then in prison. Through Paul, Onesimus became a Christian. Paul's letter in an appeal to Philemon to be reconciled to his slave, and welcome him as a Christian brother.

Chapter 1

I would prefer it if you would help me of your own free will rather than be forced to do it. So I will not do anything without your approval.

Verse 14

The Epistle to the Hebrews

The author of this epistle is unknown. Scholars are agreed that he was a Christian Jew, a Hellenist who knew the Hebrew scripture well. The epistle was written to a group of Jewish Christians, possibly those in Jerusalem, for the purpose of combating a strong tendency to return to Judaism. Its date is probably a little before A.D. 62. Though there are many uncertainties about the authorship and purpose of this epistle, it has exerted a great influence in the Christian church.

Chapter 3

You must help one another every day, so that none of you is deceived by sin and becomes stubborn, while that word 'today' in the scripture still sounds in your ear.

Verse 13

Chapter 9

It is the lot of men to die once, and after that comes the judgement.

Verse 27

Chapter 11

Faith gives substance to our hopes, and makes us certain of the realities we do not see.

Verse 1

Chapter 12

The Lord disciplines those whom he loves, and punishes everyone whom he accepts as a son.

Verse 6

Lift up your tired hands, and strengthen your trembling knees.

Verse 12

Chapter 13

Keep on loving your fellow Christians.

Remember to show hospitality even to strangers. By doing so, some have entertained angels without knowing it.

Verses 1-2

Do not live for money, and be satisfied with what you have. God has said, "I will never leave you; I will never desert you."

Verse 5

The Epistle of James

This epistle was probably written sometime before A.D. 62 or A.D. 63 by James the Just. Thus it contains many reminiscences of Jesus not found in the Gospels. It was addressed to the Jewish Christian communities outside of Palestine, warning them against substituting words for deeds.

Chapter 1

My dear brothers remember that every one must be quick to listen, but slow to speak, and slow to become angry.

Verse 19

Be assured that you act on the message and do not merely listen, for that would be misleading yourselves.

A man who listens to the message but never acts upon it is like a man who looks in a mirror and sees himself as he is.

Verses 22-23

What God the Father considers to be pure and genuine religion is this: to take care of orphans and widows in their suffering and to keep oneself from being corrupted by the world.

Verse 27

Chapter 2

As the body without the spirit is dead so also faith without actions is dead.

Verse 26

Chapter 3

No one has even been able to tame the tongue. It is uncontrollable and evil, full of deadly poison.

Verse 8

Chapter 4

Humble yourselves before the Lord, and he will lift you up.

Verse 10

You do not even know what your life tomorrow will be! What is your life? It is like a mist which appears for a little time and then vanishes.

Verse 14

Chapter 5

Above all, my brothers, do not use an oath when you make a promise. Do not swear by heaven or by earth or by anything else. Say only 'yes', when you mean yes, and 'no' when you mean no.

Verse 12

Confess your sins to one another and pray for one another, then you will be healed. A good man's prayer is powerful and effective.

Verse 16

The First Epistle of Peter

St. Peter is the probable author of this epistle. He wrote it from Rome during or soon after A.D. 64 to the many Christians, who had fled from Nero's persecution of the church and had found a haven in Asia Minor. His purpose is to inspire patience and hope in these refugees.

Chapter 1

As the scripture says, All mankind are like grass and all their glory is like wild flowers. The grass withers and the flowers fall.

But the word of the Lord remains for ever. This word is the word the gospel preached to you.

Verses 24-25

Chapter 2

You should, then, rid yourself of all evil, no jealously or sin of any kind.

Be like new-born babies, always thirsty for pure spirited milk, so that by drinking it you may grow up to save your soul.

Verses 1-2

Chapter 3

But if you suffer for your virtues, you should count yourself happy. Do not be afraid of anyone, and do not worry.

Verse 14

Chapter 4

Above everything love one another earnestly, because love covers many sins.

Be hospitable to one another without complaining.

Verses 8-9

Chapter 5

You younger men must submit yourself to your elders. You should serve each other with humility, for God resists the proud, but shows favour to the humble.

Verse 5

The Second Epistle of Peter

Scholars are not agreed as to who wrote this epistle. Many hold that it was the chief apostle of Jesus, Peter, while others are just as sure that it was someone else who merely used the name of this famous figure. While it seems to have been written from Rome shortly before Peter's death, the evidence is so confusing that it seems best to accept the letter for its value and leave questions as to its authorship and time to others.

Chapter 1

For this very reason do your best to add goodness to your faith, to your goodness add knowledge.

To your knowledge, add self-control; to your self-control, add endurance and to your endurance add godliness.

To your godliness, add brotherly affection; and to your brotherly affection, add love.

Verses 5-7

All these only confirm for us the message of the prophets. You will do well to pay attention to it because it is like a lamp shining in a dark place until the day dawns and the light of the morning star shines in your hearts.

Verse 19

The First Epistle of John

This epistle was written by an unknown author who had been influenced by the fourth Gospel. (He was at Ephesus at the time, a city where John spent a good part of his life.) The date of this letter is sometime around A.D. 100. It is called 'catholic' since it is addressed to the entire church rather than to any one group of Christians. Indeed, it is hardly a letter at all, but a sermon in which the author gives much moral and practical advice.

Chapter 1

If we say that we have no sin, we deceive ourselves, and there is no truth in us.

Verse 8

Chapter 2

Whoever does not love, does not know God, for God is love.

Verse 8

If someone says he loves God, but hates his brother, he is a liar. For if he does not love his brother, whom he has seen, how can he love God, whom he has not seen?

And this commandment comes to us from Christ: that he who loves God must also love his brother.

Verses 10-11

But you belong to God, my children, and you have the mastery over these false prophets, because he who inspires you is greater than he who inspires the Godless world.

Verse 14

Chapter 5

We can approach God with confidence because we are sure that he will listen to us if we ask him for anything that is according to his will.

He always listens to us when we ask him; as we know this is true, also know that he gives us what we ask from him.

Verses 14-15

The Second Epistle of John

The second letter of John was written by 'the Elder', 'to the dear lady and her children,' probably meaning a local church and its members. The brief message is an appeal to love one another and a warning against false teachers and their teachings.

Chapter 1

Because the truth remains in us and will be with us for ever.

Grace, mercy and peace shall be given by God the Father and Jesus Christ, the Father's Son; may they be in truth and love.

Verses 2-3

And love means following the commandments of God. The commandment, which you have heard from the beginning, is that all of us should live in love.

Verse 6

Any one who does not stand by the doctrine of Christ but goes beyond it is without God. He who stands by that doctrine has both the Father and the Son.

Verse 9

The Third Epistle of John

The third letter of John was written by 'the Elder' to a church leader named Gaius. The writer praises Gaius because of his help to other Christians, and warns against a man named Diotrephes.

Chapter 1

My dear Gaius, I pray that you prosper and enjoy good health-as I know it goes well with your soul.

Verse 2

Nothing gives me greater joy than to hear that my children live in the truth.

Verse 4

My dear friend, do not imitate what is bad but imitate what is good. Whoever does good belongs to God: but whoever does bad, has not seen God.

Verse 11

The Epistle of Jude

The letter from Jude was written to warn against false teachers who claimed to be believers. In this brief letter, the writer encourages his readers "to fight on for the faith which once and for all, God has given to his people."

Chapter 1

May mercy, peace and love be yours in full measure.

Verse 2

To the only God our Saviour, through Jesus Christ our Lord, be glory, majesty, might and authority, from all ages past, and present, and for ever and ever!

Verse 25

The Revelation of Christ to St. John

Although there are many who disagree, evidence seems to indicate that this book was written by an unknown writer called John about A.D. 95. The book is one of prophecy. It is written in figurative language and is, therefore, open to many interpretations. The basic aim of the book is to assure and strengthen a community suffering severe persecution for its beliefs.

Chapter 1

John has told all that he has seen. This is his report concerning the message from God and the truth revealed by Jesus Christ.

Verse 2

Chapter 2

Do not be afraid of the suffering to come. The devil will test you by throwing some of you into prison, and your troubles will last ten days. Be faithful to me, even if it means death, and I will give you life as the prize you have won.

If you have ears, then hear what the Spirit says to the churches, "The victorious cannot be harmed by the second death."

Verses 10-11

Chapter 3

Listen! I stand at the door and knock; if anyone hears my voice and opens the door, I will come into his house and eat with him, and he will eat with me.

Verse 20

Chapter 22

"Listen!" says Jesus, "I am coming soon! I will bring my rewards with me, to give to each one according to what he has done."

Verse 12

❑ ❑ ❑

About the Author

O.P. Ghai, a great orator, known for his communication skills, was a publisher by profession. He believed in the fundamental unity underlying the great living religions of the world and hence sought to promote religious co-existence through the written as well as the spoken word by editing a treatise, *Unity in Diversity*, which became a widely translated book in India and abroad.

A graduate of Punjab University, Lahore, who started his career as a school teacher, he founded Universal Publishers, Sterling Publishers and the Institute of Book Publishing and rose to become a member of the Executive

Committee of the International Publishers Association, a rare honour. Among his other books are a four-volume *Quest for the Fine Art of Living, Excellence in World Religions, and Golden Gift Collection.*

"I am a great admirer of your sense of dedication and remarkable enthusiasm."

-T.N. Chaturvedi

"This is a new line in which you have made such a good start, that shows the diversity of your interests. It is indeed rare to find a publisher doing both tasks successfully – publishing as well as writing."

-K.P. Bahadur

"There is a secret here, greater than that of the atom, which mankind has not yet discovered: How, out of complexity, to distil simplicity: out of knowledge, essential understanding; out of confusion, clarity. Upon its discovery will depend the survival of a humane and free society."

SIMPLIFYING
THE SCRIPTURES

Simplifying the Scriptures is a project transcreating the texts of the world's great religions in a simple language to promote personal development as well as ethnic, racial and religious harmony contributing to national integration and international understanding among the peoples of the world.

The books in the project which have just been completed are:

Unity in Diversity
With a Foreword by Dr. Mulk Raj Anand

Bhagavad Gita
With a Foreword by M.P. Pandit

Japji
With a Foreword by
Dr. Jaswant Singh Neki

Selections from the Qur'an
With a Foreword by
Prof. Rasheeduddin Khan

Selections from the Bible
(The New Testament)
With a Foreword by Fr. T.V. Kunnunkal

Other Titles in the Series

ALL YOU WANTED TO KNOW ABOUT

Parapsychology/Spiritual Sciences

- Spiritualism in Day-to-Day Life
- The Prophecies of Nostradamus
- Spirituality
- Nostradamus
- Spiritual Healing
- Dowsing
- Psychic Development
- Aura
- Hypnosis

Personal Transformation

- Practical Approach to Reiki
- Tantra Yoga
- Karma Yoga
- Jnana Yoga
- Bhakti Yoga
- Hatha Yoga
- Relaxation
- Kriya Yoga
- Meditation
- Kundalini

- Chakras and Nadis
- Happiness
- Reiki
- Mantras

Self-Help & Success
- Body Language
- Gardening
- Etiquette
- Self Motivation
- Love and Relationships
- Secrets of Magic
- As a Man Thinketh
- Vedic Mathematics
- Stress & Anger
- Secret of Success
- Feng Shui
- I Ching
- Vastushastra
- Increasing Memory Power

For complete catalogue write to:
A-59 Okhla Industrial Area, Phase-II,
New Delhi-110020.
Tel: 26387070, 2 6386209
Fax: 91-11-26383788 E-mail: ghai@nde.vsnl.net.in

Selections from the Bible

For the non-Christian reader seeking to be introduced to the New Testament, this selection is an apertif, that may well induce an appetite for the real thing, which is a flowing stream rather than periodical drops in time.

-The Hindustan Times

The devotion of the author to initiate the reader into the Bible to know the essence of the Christian faith is admirable indeed.

-The Hindu